Sara Hirsch is a London-grown [...] is a former UK Slam Champion, [...] in 2014 and she won the Europ[...] has performed at Glastonbury, h[...] UK and internationally, and has [...] Radio 2.

After the success of her award-winning debut solo show *How Was It for You?* Sara teamed up with Kiwi poet Ben Fagan with the two-hander spoken word show *Made to Measure*, which ran at the Edinburgh Fringe. The pair were also crowned runners-up in the UK National Anti-Slam the same year.

Described as 'annoyingly good' by Harry Baker, Sara's debut collection *Still Falling* was published by Burning Eye Books in 2016. *Louder Than Words* is *Still Falling*'s younger sibling: slightly rebellious, with a few hand-me-downs and not at all attention-seeking...

Sara recently received a master's degree in Creative Writing and Education and is one of a handful of trained spoken word educators working in schools and communities across the world. Sara has run workshops for Ledbury Poetry Festival, Goldsmiths University, the Royal Central School of Speech and Drama and the Museum of London as well as tutoring on the annual poetry in performance course at the National Youth Drama School of New Zealand. She was poet in residence at Lammas School & Sixth Form for two years and has presented her research at the Critical Connections Conference and in the *EAL* academic journal.

Sara's students have given up trying to teach her Snapchat, but she can be found on Twitter @sarsbars89

LOUDER THAN WORDS

To Jack

Keep writing!

SARA HIRSCH

This edition published by Bx3
an imprint of Burning Eye Books
2017

Burning Eye Books
15 West Hill, Portishead, BS20 6LG

ISBN 978-1-911570-21-9

This is a collection, a collaboration, a conversation between poems. Some are by students who are sometimes poets and most are by a poet who is sometimes a teacher.

These poems exist because of each other.

***

I am the most important

you are the most important

we are the most important.

***

Featuring poems by Sara Hirsch and students from the Orion and Goldbeaters primary schools in North London, from Lammas Secondary School & Sixth Form in Leyton, and from the performance poetry class of 2017 at the National Youth Drama School of New Zealand.

For Inky
(who found the ocean, despite the odds)

CONTENTS

AIRPLANE HEARTS

by Grace Stephenson (age 18)

Airplanes cross over my flat.
From here they are small
but noisy.

They take others
where they want to go,
full of passengers
and small bowls of sweets.

I see them as they move
through the clouds
and in to land.

Small adventures take place
just above my head.

Safety warnings are ignored
by everyone too eager to begin.

Some drink till it's bearable
and those lucky enough
to have a window sat
just watch.

I wonder if they look down at me?
If someone would notice
my control tower brain
and runway thighs?

My airplane heart
would like to fly.

WHAT THEY TEACH ME

Today I learnt that the boy
with the untucked shirt
feels more than he lets on.

All he said
was that home
is a basketball court.

All he told me
was that he
gets bounced around
one too many times.

All he admitted
was that the crowd
doesn't support the team.
That they cheer for themselves,
too loudly, it seems.

Today I learnt that the girl
at the back of the class
is struggling.

All she told me
is that she is dirt,
walked all over.

She dug her eyes deep
into the earth
when she told me this.

It didn't muddy her sentiment.

She is sediment,
sowing her seeds,
waiting to grow out
of all of this.

Out in the hallway
Toby becomes
a pressure cooker
right at my feet.

It takes four teachers
untrained in this
to become a straitjacket.

Today I learnt
that in this
sometimes classroom,
sometimes waiting room

there is a table of children
whose family
are airmail postage stamps

and they have forgotten the address
or maybe just the language
it is written in.

Just beyond the door
the only way Toby can explain
why he is the way he is
is by turning his tonsils
into razor blades
and his feet into catapults.

All he told us
is that his hurt is so deep
we should not try to help
in case we fall in too.

All that he showed us
is that the floor
will not discriminate
between stamps of feet
and those of heads.

All that he meant
remains encrypted
in his kicks.

The kid who sits on her own
tells me the clouds
are an army
waiting to attack.

Most imagine marshmallows.

I remember too well
what it felt like
when it was always
just about to rain.

FIRST DAY IN A NEW JOB

The schoolyard is a cemetery of my fear. My worries
are headstone blazers on the backs of computer-game
zombies who haunt my saunter into school. I could
bury myself alive in here. This is no place for a poet.

I need you to grab my hand and drag me through
the schoolyard graveyard after dark. Make me walk
my nightmare. When my footsteps resist, insist they
keep going, crunching over *was that a bone?* It is never a bone.

It is stick and stone words that break at my boots
and echo up my spine as I climb through the corridors
trying to find safety in staff rooms, cups of cold coffee
and the rhythm of the photocopier, tomb-like in the corner
while the ghosts haunt me, taunt me from their desks.

Let me jump at the shadow of a hundred expectant faces
in the murky moonlit hall, let them all smell my terror.
Let it fill them up, let it give them hope that even grown-ups
are afraid of the dark.

Let go of my hand and I will run through the blackboard night.
Past the trees that trip me, past the ghouls that lurk in doorways
waiting for me to pass. Past the buried books that
remind me that I don't know enough to do this.

Until I start to see glimmers of light in curious eyes that
guide me to safety. Until I remember that everyone wants
their hand held sometimes. That everyone is scared of the
dark before they get used to it,

that everything is a graveyard
until you bury your fear of it.

A SAFE SPACE

by Kassian Houben (age 17)

A safe space is the preparation
for when safety is no longer there.

It is the transition to the permeable
from the frosted glass window,
hiding outlines, pearls of colours,
to the sudden winter air,
details transpiring.

It is the ritual of change practised,
from the red of the hearth,
self-cuddle zone, soul sun bath,
to the winter garden,
an observatory.

It is a channel of creative vision
from the literal spark,
dancing, holding hands,
to the spark of closed eyes,
a mandala of ideas.

It is not forever,
but it is in this poem,
it is with you.

A safe space is the preparation
for when safety is no longer needed

or

it is the instruction, the incentive
to create safety within yourself.

NEW COLLEAGUES

I want to tell you about what happened in the classroom.
In the Wi-Fi-free war zone, where banter is a bully's best bullet
and battle-cry jibes bounce off tripping tongues
and your best bet is bite back or be broken
by cheap shots and belittling and badly built word bombs.
Boom. And you're beaten.

Can I tell you about what happened in the classroom?
In the post-break-time zoo where little monkeys
are suddenly free from their cages,
ripping up pages we printed and swinging
from tails of too much sugar
and not enough attention
and best mate primates become incubated irritated inmates.

Where we are suddenly keepers of the worst kind of secret.
Where we are cleaning out the pigsty language
and sweeping stinking statements off the ceiling,
into the mouths of impatient mammals
eager to spit them back out again.

So can I tell you what happened?

Round the table
a dozen doubters gathered.
Student soldiers studded with swearword scars
and packs of creatures
wild enough to rip your smile off and swallow it whole.

We lured them in.
Wound nooses of words
round their necks,
alphabeted traps
for them to fall into, unaware.
Drew rope ladder metaphors in the trenches
for them to climb out until they were ours.

Then it happened.

They sang tuneless songs in slang for us.
They listened to each other
because their stories were worth listening to,
they let images fall into their laps and lapped them up,
drinking poetry like Lucozade,
buzzing off the energy of what they had created.
They spoke and shared and spared us a little
of their precious attention.

A table of teenagers acted like adults
for us, for just a moment. Then the bell went.
The call to battle, feeding time at the zoo,
and the soldiers rose from their chairs,
the chimps grabbed their bags
and scampered off into the corridors
and teeth were bared
and bullets flew.

But I was there. I saw it. It happened.

The best kind of secret
is the kind that is kept
in the bottom of school bags,
in the scrape of plastic chairs
and the voices of students
who, despite what they say,

kind of
sort of

care.

GENERIC TITLE. IN BOLD. FOR EMPHASIS.

This poem hasn't got a striking first line.
It doesn't want one.

It doesn't want to draw attention to itself;
it is a shy poem, or so it wants you to think.

This poem doesn't use metaphor.
It *is* metaphor.

For the record, it could have
a striking first line if it wanted one, but it doesn't.
It doesn't think you deserve one.
Or at least that is what this poem
wants you to think.

This poem is not *like* anything.
It is not written *as if* or even *as*.
If this poem were,
it would be a different poem.
Perhaps the one you crush between your teeth
between your morning coffee
and your first slice of toast,
buttered with the kind of poetry
you need at that time of the day,
before your eyes have opened fully,
before your curtains are drawn to more than a crack
to let the day whisper its mood to you,
as you decide on yours.

But it isn't. This poem would eat that poem
for breakfast. Spitting out the clichés
and leaving them on the side of the plate
like orange pips or discarded lines
that didn't make the cut.

Perhaps, if this were not this poem
it would be the poem
that washes over you

as you shower away your sleep,
sudded with soapy similes
like
those kinds of poems often are.

Maybe it would be the poem
you don't mention to your love
because it writes you in a bad light.

Or the poem you let fester in your locker
for the cleaners to discover,
months after you left.
The key still slung lazily on your keyring
so they had to bust it open,
expecting to find a mouldy sandwich
or an unfolded uniform,
instead finding themselves laughing together
over a poem you didn't edit
because you didn't have the time.

Perhaps this poem would be like that
if it were *like* anything.

But it isn't.

Or maybe that is
exactly
what this poem

wants you to think.

ACTIONS SPEAK…

With words you can bend truths,
change minds, shape stories.

You can play with words.
Twirl them round like a spinning top,
then let them fall to the ground,
topple, into the space
where you choose to land them.

You can use my words if you like.
Rinse them, spit them and repeat them
like mouthwash, like backwash.

You can mould words
like clay, and like clay
they will set and they will stay.

Words, like scars, like DNA,
like the memory of footsteps,
are an echo of permanence,

they can get in the way.
They can build walls
quicker than hands can.

But your silence

                    your silence
is your secret weapon.
Your silence can speak
of all the reasons why you can't.
Your silence arrests me,
holds me hostage.

To your silence I am handcuffed,
forced to follow, waiting
for the time you choose
to break it.
In your silence

you can hold your peace.
Not forever, but for long enough
to cradle it, to let its quiet
crawl in and lie dormant
in your speech,
its calm caressing every intake
so that when you finally breathe words
they are not just air,
not just there to fill the space
like placeholders.

Let your silence
stand on your shoulders
and take a look at what the world
looks like from a distance.

Once you have an idea of how
to hold your peace proudly,
properly, then speak, now.

Use your silence
as well as your words
and you will have the world
at the tip of your tongue,
hanging off
holding on
dangling on your breath,
shackled to the promise of something
you have yet to say.

WORDS

by Gustavo Gomes (age 13) and Darius Postolache (age 12)

What are words? he mumbled
as his words rapidly fired out of his mouth
like that annoying person constantly clicking their pen at the back
of the class.

> All I said
> in answer was
> *potential*
> *capable*
> *strong*
> as the shots
> echoed in my ears.

Mine are not as capable as yours.
They feel left out, like damaged stock
at the back of the shop.
They feel broken,
worried they'll get it wrong,
discouraged by the thought
of being defeated.

But his words pierced through
my bullying night terrors
like a swarm of bees fighting for their hive.

The words dropped and nosedived
and flew back up and reshaped to say:

> *Your words*
> *are stronger*
> *than your velvet suit*
> *that shines*
> *in the moonlight,*
> *than your wealth*
> *which built you houses*
> *and forged you an Audi R8.*
> *They have the potential*

to piece together
answers at press conferences.
They are capable
of teaching the rules of life
to your children, or engineering
your products to sell.

When other people's words
are a bad influence
like a celebrity abusing the rules
you taught to your children
who look up to them,
don't listen.
Cut them short
like a boring film
because you are the master
of your words.

Use them wisely.

WHAT'S IN A NAME?

Before you jump to conclusions
let me assure you, this one's not for you.
This one's for the friends of friends,
the strangers and the *nice to see you again*-s.
This one's for the letter senders,
the introducers and the *have you met?*-ers.
This is for the greeters, the tweeters and the *nice to meet*-ers.
The ones who weren't listening and the *can you repeat?*-ers.

This one is not for you.

You know better than this, or at least I hope you do
and if you don't, then by the end of this one you should.
So no offence meant, OK? Got it? Good.

Right. My. Name. Is. *Sara*.

It never has been and never will be *Sarah*.
Not that I have anything against the name *Sarah*,
I know two or three *Sarah*s that I care about deeply,
but adding an H to my name is not really
the same name at all but a new one completely.
As far as I know *Sarah* is spelt with an H
whereas I spell my name simply S. A. R. A.
It's pronounced like it's spelt, so please say it that way,
unless you're American in which case it's fine,
they say the name *Sarah* but spell it like mine,
but otherwise, if I've told you it's *Sara*,
please don't call me *Sarah*, or even worse… *Zara*…

An S is an S and a Z is a Z,
they're different on paper and the way that they're said.
They're two different letters, and though neither is 'better'
you can't just discard one and use the other instead.

[dramatic pause]

You wouldn't call a *Lara Lareh*, you wouldn't call a *Tara Tarah*,
so although *Sara* and *Sarah* share a similar sound,
Sara is rarer than *Sarah*, I've found.
Sara is shorter and sweeter than *Sarah*,
like *Clara* or *calmer* or *llama* or *farmer*.
Whereas *Sarah* is longer like *sharer* or *squarer*,
the vowel's elongated from *ara* to *airer*
and while I like long words like *darer* or *carer*
or *starer* or *fairer* or *bearer* or *wearer*,
I think less can be more when it comes to a name
and although I hate to point the blame
I think it's a shame that you think
two completely different names are the same!

[awkward pause]

Oh dear... I think I just got a bit carried away.
I shouldn't let it get to me in this way, it's a common mistake,
and anyway, it's nothing personal.
I take it all back; I mean, a name's just a name,
and as Shakespeare said,
by any other I should... smell the same?

Forgive me, ignore me, I got into a state.
Call me whatever, I think both names are great.
I really don't mind what you call me, I swear.
Honestly, I really don't care!

I mean it, I'm sorry, it's one tiny letter.

Please... .call me *Sarah*...

but *Sara* is better.

AND THEY CALLED ME

by Adam Bankole (age 11)

And they called me Alex.
I'm sure I knew one, but I definitely
was not one. Sometimes, though,
it buried in my mind.
My mind is cheese
and *Alex* is the mice.

And they called me safe.
No, I wasn't locked up
or hidden
but generous and giving.

And they called me different.
Yes, it's true, I fly in my mind,
a hole of jelly and marshmallows.

I open the prize of present and future
after tossing the past to oblivion.

The disease of joy melts my heart.

My mother is my lighter
and I am the firework
shot afar to my dreams.

The sound of laughter
crushes my brain
while the happy sensation
devours my heart.

And they called me me,
and I liked it.

MY NAME

by a Year 9 EAL group

My name is a nervous tornado
destroying the city of Kabul.

My name is a tired grey Jeep
driving from Afghanistan to London.

My name is the Khalifa tower in Dubai,
too rich, a beautiful triangle in the ocean of sky.

My name is a happy smile stretching
across London tower blocks.

My name is a question mark.

RUINS

They tell you that you are using broken English,
that your tongue is faulty,
in need of replacement.

I don't want to put words into your mouth
in case you don't like the taste,
but it is not broken, that which is yet to be built.

Your laptop is broken.
Stutters awkwardly through conversations
with Google, too shy to finish.

Divorcing document from hard drive,
only memories remain and the alimony
demanded when you send it away to be fixed.

Your glasses broke once, cracked vision,
unhinged perspective. You taped them up
and hoped for a refund.

Your trust has been broken many times.
Bombed out, reduced to dust,
then bricked back up,

with wider cracks
than before the lies
came marching through.

But your sentences are not falling apart.
They cannot send them back
to where they came from.

They cannot demand
their money back
for something you have yet to structure.

So when your conversations turn into hostage situations,
do not hold your tongue at gunpoint
like it is some kind of victim.

Your words are not weapons
and your speech is not ruined,
is not ruptured, is not broken.

You cannot mend something
if it is not yet strong enough
to do damage.

I AM A REFUGEE

by Maariya Ahmad (age 12)

I am the wilting flower that needs
a little water to flourish.
I am the hopeless parcel,
delivery constantly postponed.
I am the frozen polar bear who has to leave
their home at the risk of never returning.
I become the centre
of two conflicting countries.
I am the flying leaf who needs a branch
to be their quilted blanket on a bitter winter's day.
I am the flower without a stem,
I am the scars on my hand, I am the prey.
I am the desolate debris that clings to my feet.
I am covered in rubble and blood.
I am the street rat
searching for food in the bins.
I am the gift that was short-lived.
I am the girl without a Monday morning
Mum lecture about chores.

Every step
I am at risk.

STRENGTH

by Nabeel Khan (age 13)

Because I have had nothing, I am generous.
Because I have been mistreated, I am kind.
Because I have been lied to, I am honest.
Because I have been foolish, I am wise.
Because I have been hurt, I am happy.
Because I have made mistakes, I have succeeded.

I WISH, or HOW TO EXPLAIN BREXIT TO TEENAGERS

I wish I could think straight.
Bend these decisions back on themselves,
snap them into clarity,
unfold the image I have of this country
and smooth out the creases.

I wish I was braver.
I am stood at the door of the plane,
parachute strapped, doing the opposite of jumping.

I wish I knew all the words.
I wish I could spell them.
I wish I had shoes like that.
I wish we had known better.
I wish it wasn't like this.

I wish we weren't hiding
behind someone else's bravado.
He is stood at the front of the class,
PowerPoint poised,
doing the opposite of jumping.

We wish we had learnt how to land safely,
so we weren't worried about our knees jamming.
If we had learnt how to land properly,
if we had the right shoes
and just the right angle
we could cushion our ankles,
but we spent too long folding ourselves
into a structure for someone else to rely on
that we forgot to practise our free fall.

They will tell you to enjoy the jump.
I will tell you to relish the unknown.
But what do we know?
We can't even think straight
and we are the opposite of jumping

I wish I knew what to tell you.
I really do. Maybe one day,
when they bend their knees and launch,
they will be in a better position to tell us what falling feels like.

Until then
try doing more
than just wishing.
That's what I would do
if I were you.

If I were you
I would jump at the chance.

MATHS

a group poem written by 11-year-olds

I wish I was better at maths.
If the world was a square
it would be easier to share.
I wish the world was equal,
but it is not divided properly.
The correct word to use is *unbalanced.*

I wish it was possible to even out the ratio
of rich and poor.
I wish I was better at maths.
I wish I could work out
the EU, but I am no good at algebra.

I wish I was old enough to vote for our future
but they are judging us by numbers;
one plus one does not equal eighteen.
I wish they hadn't minused us from our freedom.
I wish I was better at maths.

I wish there wasn't fractions
so there would be no remainders.
No remaining refugees.
Refugees on the other side
of the divide sign border.

Sixteen divided by five equals
three remainder one.
There will always be a remainder.
I wish I could be a mathematics pro

but it takes more practice.

BELONGING

My eyes belonged to my father
before I belonged to him.

My hands belong to gloves and pens
my eye belongs to a contact lens
my heart belongs to books
to friends
to the sea

my hand belongs to you sometimes
and my mind belongs to me.

My legs belong to my feet most days
they belong to the road
they belong to the waves
and the waves belong to memories
and those belong to us.

My lips belong to my favourite words
and my words belong to everyone
and my words don't belong to anyone
and my words belong to silence
and my words belong to

and my words belong.

EXCERPTS FROM 'BELONGING'

by a group of 14-year-olds. This poem was written for the Critical Connections Multilingual Digital Storytelling Project 2017. It is written for multiple voices.

I belong to my country, my city, my phone.
My phone is my security guard;
like a best friend, it is there when I am lonely.
My country is an artist; it paints the turquoise of my blood.

I belong to Facebook likes and Instagram.
Instagram is loud, a spectacular library
capturing your five-star moments.
You can browse everyone's fake covers,
skim-read their best bits,
check out what they're doing,
then double tap.
Why do some people's books
get borrowed more than mine?

Dear social media.
Stop trying to make us who we are not.
We don't like it.

I don't belong to posh,
to the Queen's language,
to Britain.
This country is a difficult exam I haven't studied for.

I belong to Nigeria, to Jamaica, to Pakistan.
I am the representation of green.

I belong to Turkey.
I am the Hilal, I have the blood of the red,
I am the sound of the clear blue sea,
I have the perfume of you. I smell like adventure and youth.

Sensin benim evim [you are my home].
Sensi benim tarihim [you are my history].

Sensin benim geleceğimsin [you are my future].
Ama seni sen yapan benim [but I make you you].

These are our stars that are shining,
this is our flag that is waves,
this is my nation that won't sink.

Aš priklausau Lietuvos žaliųjų sodaus
[I belong to Lithuania's green gardens].

I belong to being foreign in both places.
I belong to an unknown language;
hearing it is like trying to work out
a difficult science equation.

I belong to friendship;
my friends are my life jackets.
I belong to family, to equality.

I do not belong to other people's opinions
and their opinions do not belong to me.

MY BROTHER (WHO USED TO HAVE RED HAIR)

by Kassian Houben (age 17)

Look at the red spikes,
fiery arrows stuck in the sand
where he stood.

He is a bold cactus,
strong-willed in a drought,
stubborn in his dry element,
no spikes left for future, or past,
just the now,
his green voice rasping
from red storms.

He has Down syndrome.

If he could write this poem
he would say:

You are the cactus, I the outside world.
I have lost all my spikes
so if you receive any from me
remember where they came from.

You are the cactus,
I the outside world.

PRESENT

I keep my father in the folds of his knitwear.
I keep November in the neckline
and his surname in the colour.

You cannot get a darker green and still call it green.

I remember when I would watch my mother sew his name
into my school uniform, head bent in concentration,
patience threaded into her focus, the likes of which
I wouldn't know for years. I wore his name with pride.

Carved it cursively onto exercise books,
answered to it in the register, always thankful to be
near the front, never waiting like the Woods or the
Thompsons for my turn to come around.

Atkinson
Bagri
Broydo
Currell
Delaney
Defreitas

       Green.
Present
       I would call into the classroom.

Sometimes we would joke, shout things like
Christmas tree or *Rudolph*, not understanding
that the game was not to name festive things.
That present meant *here*, that we existed,
that we were proof of us.

Introductions went
         Sara no H
         Green no E
         just like the colour.
His name would sit on my tongue, heavy,
like extravagant family dinners and Christmas
when everyone was present.
Now it lies printed on my bank card like a secret.

It is passports and payslips (the other me is self-employed).
I use it only when I have to, like tax avoidance of a past
that no longer fits.

Each November I pull my father out from his drawer,
dust off another year without him and pull his name
over my head.

Sometimes his jumper is a hug.
Sometimes it is strength,
and sometimes just a vintage item
for people to blindly compliment,
unaware that it is not an attempt at fashion.

I tell them it was a present.
That it belonged to someone else before me.
That it is proof that he was.

I wear him through the month he stopped existing
like armour, like a shroud, like evidence.

His jumper is my mood that month

          you cannot get a darker green and still call it green.
I wear him as we approach another Christmas
without his presence, to ward it off, like Scrooge,
like Grinch, I steal back the years, I steal back
my name. I wear it for a while, try it on for size.

It feels like my mum has sewn me into it
and with her patience I make it through the month.
Then he goes back in his drawer, neatly folded, waiting,
like the Woods, for his name to be called.

          I keep him waiting.

I keep him in the folds of his knitwear.

I keep November in the neckline
and his surname in the colour.

GAMES

by Rahmoan Williams (age 13)

Admit it, you were playing
hide and seek with me.

Thinking it's a great place to hide
six feet deep under the ground.

How long were you planning to stay there?
You found me before I could find you.

It's not fair. You were cheating,
you can't just hide somewhere
and never come back.

At this point I don't know
if it's about me or you, Grandad.

SUGAR COOKIES

by Caitlyn Esson (age 17)

My mother has never been round. Or soft.
Never been shortbread or sugar cookies.
I have grown up watching her try to squeeze
herself into this mould, this cookie cutter,
trying to file down the edges that don't fit.

But the overflow is too great, too vast
the sea in which I've drowned again
and again. My mother has been all edges,
concaving cheeks dragged in by all the things
she wants to say and sparrow's bones.
She just wants to fly.

The little girl with the blue eyes
and too many questions holds her back,
grasping her hand with sticky fingers
and asking why her shoulder blades stick out
like the knives she isn't allowed to touch and
why she never faces me when she's changing.

My mother makes the perfect porridge,
tap water and brown sugar never tasted so
sweet. She has the calloused hands of a
working man and I could watch them for hours,
in awe as she kneads and folds and turns pain
into poetry.

Why can't I?

I've never been much good at kneading
and shirtsleeves always seem too long.
I keep folding them over twice and getting lost
somewhere in the middle.

I call out for help and she comes to unravel me
with floury hands and bottle cap wrists.
I've never liked sugar cookies.

SOCIETY'S WISH

by Iqra Shahid (age 13)

Portraying the world through our clouded eyes,
as if the world's a place to be forgotten.
Treading upon the shattered glass,
scrutinising the pale dead skin
and beady eyes that stared back at you.
No hips, no bones to be seen.

We've been taught to despise ourselves,
a chorus of egotistical narcissists,
we're shunned for our spiteful confidence
as they feed us our own flaws.
Stare daggers into the ever-shattered mirror
with your glossy eyes closed,
deny myself the right to be shown myself,
because I didn't dare want to insinuate beauty
in regards to something as insulting
as my body.

But we always end up with our heads
between our knees, because the only place
we'll ever truly feel safe is curled up within skin
we are bred to hate.

In regards to a self-mutilating circus
we have painted ourselves clowns in,
in a humanity where society-conformed women
willingly scavenge upon stories to find that
societal 'justifiable' gown,
but haven't a clue where to find joy
or how to wear happiness.

I strive to find the me that loves me
but I can never find her,
'cause I'm buried six feet under
the congested soil of society's wish.
Skinny, pretty, skinny, pretty.

First words fulfilling the petty expectations
a madman established,
where have we been?
Drowning under the narcissism
and pain we've been taught to claim,
but are we still drowning?

We don't live to acclaim to the credentials
established, our words aren't drowning, we are.

We aren't defined by our waistlines,
or the bones protruding from our skin,
'cause no miracle cream can smooth over the
passion and beauty we possess within.

You can't allow these malicious comments
to pollute our mentalities,
you better examine the miracle of your existence,
you are a treasure, whether you want to believe it
or not, and maybe that's what we should start
looking for.

ALL ABOUT MUM

by Adam Yussuf (age 11)

Positive, clever and kind,
the angel floating above me
when I am scared.

The provider who picks me up
from school
and feeds me lovely lunch.

Providing,
sheltering.

Mum, mum, my mum.

Mum is the one,
the fluffy marshmallow,
cushions me when I fall.

A fiery volcano
when I do something naughty.

An illuminating moon
when the night is dark.

An indestructible element
that will stay with me forever.

LIKE WILDFIRE

This poem was written for the Museum of London in February 2017 as part of 'Poetry Aflame', a special commission for which Sara worked with members of the pubic to generate material before writing a poem inspired by the responses. The theme was the Great Fire of London.

No one knows exactly who started the rumour.
Some say it was the baker, but we know
it doesn't really matter.

A rumour is not about the source but the spread.
Like disease, its power is not in the
first bitten, but in counting the dead.

***

I was always just supposed to be a whisper,
a rumbling in the gutter, a mutter under
London's breath, blending in, part of the clutter,

but a lot of people like to chatter, and I
scattered like sparks from one mouth to another.
It's not my fault they built themselves so close together.

I grew louder. Until the streets hummed red with mentions
of my name. My ears were burning bright as each house
flamed gold in jaundiced shame

and then the wind changed

and suddenly this humble mumble
was given a gust of confidence.

I took the inhalation gifted to me by the breeze
and I coughed and I wheezed and I billowed
and I blew. Flew, through every wooden door.

I was a scarlet scandal, volcanic gossip
like you've never heard before, an unstoppable
explosion of *did you hear?* loosed like a lion's roar.

I was music, electric, buzzing under skin,
I was a proud peacock showing off
to anyone who let me in. I was a warrior,

I was brave, I caught on like a Mexican wave,
I pulsed like blood through the city's veins,
I was the circus animal escaped from its cage.

I was laughter, I was hunger, I was rage.
Don't you recognise me? Are you sure?
Look closer, through the smoke,
trust me, we've met before.

In the blaze of a bitter word
or the crackle of a callous cackle,
every time you've scrunched your face,

every furious flicker of your tongue.
London has always been an angry place.
I'm nothing new, I just joined in the race.

You called me *great*.

I'm what you wanted,
I'm your morbid fascination,
don't you dare weep in my wake.

***

So, before you tell your children
of a sleeping city savaged by slander,
tell them the truth behind my name.

The rumour is nothing
without those that spread it.
I am not the one to blame.

MUD

by Skirmante Gvazdziauskaite (age 13), April Bowles and Hamza Akhtar (both age 14)

I am mud.

I smell fruity fresh after my daily shower.
I feel gritty, like scree sliding down a mountain.

I am made of bombed-out buildings,
roses, lemons and vegetables planted in Pakistan
that need me to grow.

I am made of vegetables by the mud path in Lithuania.
I am sweaty from the toil
of workers after wars, rebuilding, replanting.

I am deciding which trees are dead
and which are going to bloom.

I am digging with my hands and giving
a child to the ground.
I will watch it grow with a parent's support
until it can live by itself.

But one day I will sit under the shade
of this tree and eat the fruit that it births.

I am boredom in the backyard.
I have ruined a dress, mother scolding
look at the mess, sent to bed,
to a dark place and denied the light
and *wait till your father sees this!*

I am the mud of my homeland.
I give gifts to the workers
and the animals that eat the grass,
I taste of badly mashed up rice.

I become New York streets.
Cops and robbers forge me into meatball bullets,
bullies carry me in school shirts
to be thrown like weapons
into the mouths of their teenage targets.

I am mud.

I am the magnetic pull of the earth,
attracting everyone who needs
a piece of land,
giving life to the tree, it is my duty.

I have seen everything.
I am the only one who knows how the dinosaurs looked,
I've seen the people running in the trenches,
I *was* the trenches.

I saw the river running free, doing whatever it wanted,
become a canal, always flowing
the same way.

I was fun while it lasted.

Everyone thinks that I'm just dirt under your fingernails,
but I will wash off easy,
what is all the fuss?

I am mud

and all the legends are buried in me.

DAISY

It's a Friday afternoon in March and
we're playing catch at Paddington Rec
    with a hacky sack. Because we're poets
    and while the rest of the world works
        and waits for the weekend to roll in,
        we have nowhere else to be but here.
She throws to me and I catch myself
dreaming; while my hands have been
    tied, my mind has been leaning like
    Jenga. One image stacked impossibly
    on another, storing up the thoughts that
    got caught in the blur of my day and
        saving them before I forget to remember.
        I have one eye on the ball and one in my
    mind and as my mind's eye minds my
    mind I find I have time to really, really
    think. And as I haul her the ball, my
    thoughts are forming a tower so tall,
        I'm worried it could wobble and topple
        at any minute. One more building block
    of anticipation, of guilt at a morning of
    unadulterated procrastination, one more
    Friday frustration or flustered flirtation
    with the idea of doing my tax return,
    or my blundering bank balance, or my
    car insurance, will be enough to ensure
    its crumbling, tumbling demise. So I keep
    my eyes wide and a bounce in my stride,
    as the ball flies between us like an unspoken
    reassurance that with all this going on inside,
    my tower won't topple, because I have a
    friend like her. And we've been throwing
    for ten minutes now, without stopping
    or dropping the ball, and we both know
        that as long as we keep going,
        my mental Jenga tower won't fall.
Because in this space, with the metronome
beat of *throw, catch, throw, catch, throw,* I know

I can sort my thoughts from
       the top down,
       put the worries back
       in their box along
       with my frown and we
       throw, catch, throw,
       catch, throw and I go slowly.
Prise each wooden building block of
doubt from the pile and let it linger
       in my head awhile, before it's filed away
       and we *throw, catch, throw, catch,* throw as I
       methodically deal with my *bottom of the*
              bucket, out of luck but suck it up and
              take it kind of day until my tower
              has been
                  broken
                        down
                        bit
                        by
                        bit.

No longer leaning like Pisa,
       it's now easier to choose a
       brick from the middle and seize it,
or leave it for another day without
worrying about it rocking and falling
if I should accidentally knock it. She
senses this and without a word puts
the ball back into her trouser pocket
and we walk back in silence, our smiles
showing that we don't need words.
Because between us the ball is still going,
she is still *throwing* me glances as if to say
I know you needed that and I am still *catching*
her eye with a nod of *thanks.* Everyone needs
a friend like that and a Friday in the park
playing catch with a hacky sack.

ROALD DAHL

I come from Snozzcumbers
and foxes as fantastic
as the voices Mum gave them
when she brought them to life
under lamplight.

I come from wanting my medicine
to be a bit more marvellous
and marvelling at Matilda's magic,
making Mum do the voices;
I'm right and you're wrong.
I come from the Oompa Loompa song.

I come from wishing my Wonka Bar
would grant me gold and from being told
my rhymes were revolting.

I come from feeling like a champion
to feeling like a twit.
I come from a great glass lift
of nostalgia vaulting through adventures
I haven't grown out of yet.

I come from chokeys and giants,
and choking on the most giant peaches I could get.

I come from Mum reading bedtime stories
to lunch break dips into *Kiss Kiss*.
Adult lips curling round new voices
I do for myself now,
never too proud to read it out loud,
try out the way each character sounds.
After all, these worlds are where so many
of our own voices were found.

THE ROALD DAHL MUSEUM AND STORY CENTRE

The following two poems were specially commissioned 'Big Birthday Poems' written for the Roald Dahl Museum & Story Centre in September 2016, for 'Roald Dahl 100'. Sara spent the day working with members of the public in and around the museum and wrote these in response to their ideas.

OLD FRIEND

Walk the trail to discover
a national treasure,
shining golden in his grave
from a ticket saved.

Pause to admire
chocolate box cottages
propped up by
book spines
and revolting lines,
cemented from a century
of half-remembered rhymes.

A sweetly slender shadow
slips between gifted gates,
waits silently at the end
of a caramel queue,
then sneaks through
with fizzy footsteps
and disappears from view.

Did you notice how it leaned
towards the open window
to let the dreams fall through?

Stand opposite
red and white pumps,
where red kites jump
from peachy cloud

to chokey tree.
Ask, *If he looked up,*
is this what
the champion of the world
would see?

She approaches the counter
clutching books like door handles,
grips tight to the adventures
she hasn't opened yet,
lets her mind abseil down pages
catching words as they hurricane past.

The shadow casts a toothless grin,
then whispers away
before you notice him.

He shimmers past
while we are
concocting stories;
marvellous medicines
for busy minds.

But look closely,
if you can.

Is there something
in the way
the shadow
stoops
as it follows?

The way it
dances

round libraries
like a secret
only the books can see?

Notice how the shadow
tickles the stairs
familiarly
as it climbs out of sight,
hugging
the faded footsteps
of a smiling old man
with stories at his lips
and magic in his eyes,
who you
might
just
recognise.

LEGACY

He still gets emails, you know.

Answers them from the past,
imparts imagination
into every typed reply.

He lives in bricks
and bookmarks now,

he didn't really die.

THE LEAP

My fear still wears her hair in pigtails.
Her dress is torn and ripped with age,
held up by a petticoat of hand-me-down excuses,
and her pale whisper is frayed from overuse.

I convince her to the top of the mountain
and she follows with a begrudging shuffle
of shy, unsure steps. She's never been this high.
I tie a bungee rope around her middle and I
push. Somewhere an audience are screaming
the descent. Fear ambulance-sirens as she drops.

She whips her arms out and cautiously catches
the choking surface of the water. She quickly carves
a message and lets it drown. *Je ne regrette rien*
echoes in the ripples that remain, as she falls
perilously back up to meet me at the peak.

Rope wishes it hadn't tied itself so tightly
to the top. That it had maybe risked a little more give,
that it had left a little room to unravel. Fear knows
no different. She wraps her trembling arms around
my waist and wastes no time in telling me she missed me,
through vibrating tumble drier teeth. I ask her
what it was like in the water. She buries her face
in my neck and sinks her tumble driers into my tendons,
tying us together in a strangled knot. *Cold*, she mutters
in response. *But refreshing. You should try it sometime.*
I'd love to, I think as she sinks in her teeth. *If only you'd let me.*

WATERFALL – A MINOR MISUNDERSTANDING

It is an Antipodean autumn afternoon
but your feet spring up the mountain
as melodically as May might suggest.
Your toes tickle with the trill and whistle
of the water, which crescendo crashes,
splashes a concerto of cold that cackles
at your legs. The surface reflects the sun,
an out-of-tune temptation, a lesson in deceit.
Note how the dragonfly hovers in admiration
but, with knowing avoidance, does not touch.
You shudder, but you stay.

NATURE'S SONG

by Stephen Myrint (age 11)

Take the whisper of the river
the thunder of the sea
the echo of the songbird
the rustle of the tree
the howling of the blizzards
the purring of the cat
the shudder of the earthquake
the whisper of the gnat
the strike of the lightning
the singing of the sun
the music of the moonrise
and mix them one by one
until all the notes are silver
and all the chords are gold
then give your gift of laughter
to the sick, the sad and the old.

CORRESPONDENCE

In response to the news headline 'Bacon made of salmon to be sold in UK supermarkets'. This is a found poem, compiled from very real emails and texts that are definitely not made up. Published with permission from the subjects.

17th July 2010 – Email

Dear bacon,

I'm a massive fan of yours. You might not remember me, of course, but we did meet once, in an old pub kitchen, we were there for lunch – you were wrapped round chicken. It was a while ago though so I did look different.

But I wanted you to know how great I think you look, how you're so much streakier than sausage and so much easier to cook. And I want you to know that whatever you think, you're cured, calm and collected and look great in pink. And that while you may be no chop you're so much stronger than ham, and just how impressed I am at how you stood up for yourself that time against gammon. Anyway, that's all really.

Regards,
a very star-struck salmon.

25th September 2010 – Email

Dear salmon,

I'm terribly sorry for the late reply, it's been non-stop since late July. But thank you so much for your kind little note. I do remember you and the brief time we spoke and I have to say that I really am flattered, no one was that nice since cod and to be honest, she was battered! So thanks, keep well and nice to hear from you.

Love bacon.
P.S. You look great in pink too!

13th April 2011 – Email

Dear salmon,
It was great to see you briefly today, and thanks for your advice, I agree that the fat kind of does get in the way. So I've decided to drop it and try going solo. Anyway, just thought you might want to know. You were right that I'm better off just me. So cheers, speak soon.

Sincerely, B.

15th April 2011 – Email

Hi,

It was good seeing you too and good, that sounds like an excellent move. Perhaps, if you fancy, we could get together sometime? For a chat or something, but if you're busy it's fine. So yeah, let me know if you ever want to meet… or fish. LOL. Sorry, couldn't resist.

Lots of love, S.

P.S. Here's my number so drop me a text.

18th April 2011 – Text

Hi
Bacon here, are you free next week?

Yeah, how's Tuesday?

Tuesday's great.

Perfect. 6pm? Can't wait.

I will pick you up then. It's a date.

19th October 2013 – Text

Hey.
Film starts at 8, potato just text, he's going to be late. But I'm heading over now cos I don't want to miss it. See you there. I love you, salmon. Three kisses.

21st January 2014 – Text

I've been thinking. I know this is out of the blue
but you spend a lot of time at mine anyway
so how would you like to move in?
We could test it for a week, like a trial thing?
And if it works we can see what happens?
Have a think. YAY EXCITING!
Lots of love, salmon.

21st October 2014 – Email

Hey baby,
I just wanted to say, I'm sorry that people reacted in that way.
We've done nothing wrong and our love's not a crime, it's just
that it's new, so we must give them time. And we know it's real,
so let them call us fake; like you said, what's the difference
between us and tuna steak?

Keep strong, my darling, hope being sushi makes you feel better
and if you're lucky, tonight, we can get smoked together.

Winky face.

I love you.
I'll see you at home.

Love B.

Kiss kiss kiss

                                        Sent from my iPhone.

I WANT

I want to be your status
so you can update me every minute.
I want to be your candy crush
or at least I'll help you win it.

I need to be your Twitter feed.
I'll feed you facts that you will swallow.
You'll be hooked, with bated breath;
I'll take the lead and then you'll follow.

I want to be your microphone,
'cause you might phone me on Skype.
I want to be your keyboard
because you're just my type.

Oh, let me be your charger
to give you energy when you crash,
let me be your screen protector
to protect ya when you smash.

I won't cash you in for a smarter model,
I won't lash out when you're out of 4G
and I won't judge your phone by its cover;
you can be anything you want to USB.

I want to Go and play Pokémon with you,
to be the GPS to your street,
but despite seeming lofty
I'm no micro-softy;

I will control-alt-delete if you cheat!

WILL YOU?

by Anonymous (age 12)

Will you let me be the book
you pick up when you're bored?

Will you let me be your phone case
so you can hold me all day?

Will you let me be the code to your Wi-Fi connection,
so you can wait for me to load?

I'll be the backup to your iPhone
so we can sync our memories.

I'll be the football socks to your football boots
so I can be wrapped around you to give you

luck when you play. Will you let me be
the ink to your pen while you write all day?

Will you let me be the paper you write your essay on
so you can focus on me all night?

Will you let me be the star you put on your Christmas tree,
to guide your way?

If rain was kisses I'd send you showers.
If love was a person, I'd send you me.

MAKE US SOMETHING

by Amberleigh Rose (age 16)

He keeps staring at the sky
trying to take hold of it,
touch it, cradle it.
He wonders why the sky
doesn't want to be taken care of.

You have heard I'm smart, right?
Really smart, don't you like smart boys?
Don't you want someone nice to take care of you?

The sky keeps making storms
hoping he'll catch on
she doesn't need hands
to conjure currents,
she doesn't need a knife
to carve at mountain faces.

But he tells all the other hes
that someone must be meddling
with the weather
because the sky he knows,
no, the sky he knows is too blue,
too pretty to do that.

Lately, the trees
have been whispering to the sky.

He keeps trying to take us too,
says he can make us something wonderful,
something useful.
Do you think we can trust him?

The sky winces, remembering what it was like
to have holes cut out of her
just so that he could have light.
But the trees have already made up their mind.

They lie at his feet.

Make us something.

His cheeks split in two,
hands ripping and tearing
at all their loose branches,
all their ugly bits.

Make us something.

The sky turns horror,
the sky turns black hole,
the sky turns—

oh sky, are you jealous?

WHAT A WAY TO MAKE A LIVING

I meet you at Natalie's birthday
in a Soho swanky, far-too-fancy bar.
You know who you are,
you're the friend of a friend
with the flamboyant tie
and the pinstripe perfect suit,
the 'corporate guy'.
I ask your name and you reply
with a confident *Simon,*
but you can call me Si,
and I sigh to myself and try to like you.

I order another drink and so do you and then
comes the question: *So... what do you do?*
And for a second I consider lying,
telling you I work in admin, but you're
staring at me and smiling and there's
no point in denying it and before I know it
I'm replying with: *I'm a children's entertainer.*
And I know you want to laugh, most people do,
and then, so predictably, you look at me and frown;
So... you're a clown?

And it's in that moment
that I want to say this...
You know on Sunday morning
when you're snoring in your bed,
recovering from your nine-to-five?
Well, instead, I drive to a village hall
somewhere off the M25 and when I arrive
I'm awaited with bated breath;
Alison's turning five!

And yes, I dress up, and no, I don't wear
the makeup but I do have massive shoes.
And yes, I know the Hokey Cokey inside out
and even though I know it's not really
what it's all about, for two hours on a Sunday,

for me, it kind of is, and for these kids
it pretty much sums up what life is
and if you listen to the words
it really should be what life's about
– you have to put your *whole self in* in life
to get your *whole self out.*
Do you put your whole self in, Simon?
Because I do, and when I do
I shake it all about!

And yes, you correctly assume that I make balloons,
but not just any balloons. I can make a bike
out of balloons. And for Alison that is literally
the best thing she can hope for and I make that happen.
I give a five-year-old the best thing she can imagine
before you've even had your breakfast.

I can sing all the words to 'I Like to Move It, Move It'
and if that's not a skill, well, I'd like to see you do it.
And yes, I have a degree, but I also have 'conga lines' and
'magic' on my CV and yeah, I know nothing about IT
but I am fully qualified in puppetry.
I can limbo dance and disco dance
and I *can* do the can-can dance,
dressed as a princess,
for four minutes straight,
whilst blowing bubbles
and simultaneously making sure
that none of the kids touch my stuff,
or steal my stuff, or break my stuff,
or kick me, or each other.
In other words, I can multitask
and before you ask,
yes, I can make water disappear
and just to be clear,
I love my job.
I mean, I get to play on a daily basis

and judging by the look on the children's faces,
I'm pretty good at it.

And it's that look that makes me want to do it.
That *happy and you know it*
and *you really want to show it* reaction.
I mean, talk about job satisfaction!

But I don't say any of that.

I never do.

I normally just look down at the ground
and nod and mumble,
Yeah, yeah, I'm just a clown.

WHAT DO YOU WANT TO BE?

To be read aloud, ideally in a primary school assembly, in the playground or in front of the mirror.

If I asked you what you want to be when you grow up, hands up if you would say *fire fighter?*

What about *police officer? Scientist? Astronaut? Doctor? Lawyer? Artist? Teacher? Explorer?*

Hands up if you'd say *rich?*

That's great. But it doesn't really answer the question: *what do you want to be?*

Hands up if you want to see the world someday? Astound yourself with waterfalls that crash like cars or smell cities in spices and saltwater that take your nostrils hostage?

Who wants to be shooting stars? To fly like rockets and scream past Jupiter or Mars?

Hands up if you want to be brave? Rescue cats from trees and babies from burning buildings,
your name in newspapers for everyone to see?

Hands up if you want to be free? To let your boots beat your path for you, not tread the one that others do?

Hands up if you want to be happy? Your smile a stamp in your passport of every place you've ever used it, or a Valentine's card from everyone who has caused it?

Hands up if you want to be unique? A four-leafed clover in a field of three, a fingerprint that only you can claim, a pebble on the beach like no other, eroded by the sea?

Hands up if you want to be the name people remember?

Hands up if you want to be the good decisions?

The fun decisions?

Your own decisions?

Do you want to be the Ace of Spades? To be the top of the rollercoaster, or the front of the parade?

Who wants to be a raindrop, delicate as a flower? Or would you rather be the cloud that makes it, full of strength and power?

Can I tell you a secret?

When I look at you I see doctors and writers and pilots and mothers and actors and athletes
and so many others.

But I also see raindrops and race cars, smiles and stars and clouds and trees and mountains and bees. I see continents and castles and kaleidoscope dreams. I see parachutes and promises and salmon swimming fast upstream.

I see what it really means to ask the question
what do you want to be? But enough about me,

tell me, what do *you* see?

IN RESPONSE

by students from the UK and New Zealand aged 10 - 17

I want to be a sewing machine
stitching people's lives together.

I want to be an artist
who creates a masterpiece
as my paint brush
slowly walks against the smoothness
of my wonderful white canvas.
I want to be a pilot
up in the air,
my wings running.

I want to always have
a smooth landing.

Zainab (age 10)

***

I am a runners-up award.
A congratulations for trying.
A silver trophy to match the tongue.
I have never won.

I am that video game classic you used to play,
that nostalgic refreshment,
do you remember me?

I am an empty room.
I am alone.
I am cold
I am shouting
can you hear me?
I am an unsolvable equation,
the broken-down car that still tries to run,
God's scribble he couldn't quite erase.

Ed Howell (age 17)

***

I am a soldier,
I am a warrior,
I am a shield
who would do
whatever it takes
to protect
the ones I love.

I am a photographer.
I am social media,
I am a fan
who takes photos of their heroes
and posts them on Instagram,
like a spy
with eyes like a tiger
hungrily eyeing their prey.

I am a story.
I am a fantasy world
trapped in a book.

I am a calculator,
I am a maths problem,
I am a test paper
fuming with answers.

Elsa (age 10)

***

I am not a bedtime story.
There is no princess inside this body
begging to be saved.

I am not the girl
whose face crinkles up
like paper
when she smiles.

I am a polka dot poem
playing with your emotions
and spending too long in the shower,
untangling stories from my hair
and watching them float down the drain.

If you look closely,
you can see the patchwork quilt
of fairy tales
I stitch into my skin.

Tahlia Lawton (age 17)

***

Sometimes I sit and wonder what to be,
I have secrets concealed under
my blankets, you see.
I am a spectacular star
hidden in a faraway land,
a chamber where secrets
are locked tight.
During my dreams, I hear them barking to escape.

Ibrahim (age 10)

ACKNOWLEDGEMENTS

Versions of the following poems first appeared in Sara Hirsch's debut collection *Still Falling*, published by Burning Eye Books in 2016: 'First Day in a New Job', 'New Colleagues', 'Generic Title. In Bold. For Emphasis', 'Present', 'Daisy', 'The Leap', 'What a Way to Make a Living'.

'Like Wildfire' was commissioned by the Museum of London in 2017 for 'Poetry Aflame'. A version can be found on their website: https://www.museumoflondon.org.uk/discover/poetry-aflame-verse-inspired-great-fire. It was written with help from the public.

'Old Friend' and 'Legacy' were commissioned by the Roald Dahl Museum & Story Centre as 'Big Birthday Poems' for Roald Dahl 100. They were written in response to a day of workshops with members of the public and are displayed on their website: http://www.roalddahl.com/blog/2016/september/big-birthday-poem. The poems were used with permission from the museum.

The following poems were written by students at the National Youth Drama School of New Zealand in 2017: 'Airplane Heart', 'A Safe Space', 'My Brother (who used to have red hair)', 'Sugar Cookies', 'Make Us Something', parts of 'In Response'. They were published with permission from the poets.

The following poems were written during workshops with Sara at the Orion Primary School and Goldbeaters Primary School in North London and have been published with permission: 'All About Mum', 'Nature's Song', parts of 'In Response'.

The following poems were written by students at Lammas School & Sixth Form during Sara's time as poet in residence. 'Words', 'My Name', 'I am a refugee', 'Strength', 'Maths', 'Games', 'Mud', 'Will You?' They have all been published with permission.

'Mud' was written by Sara Hirsch and students in spoken word club at Lammas School & Sixth Form for the 'Tales from the Marshes' project in collaboration with Siobhan O'Neill.

'Belonging' was written for the Critical Connections II Project 2017 in partnership with Goldsmiths University, the Museum of London, the British Museum, the Paul Hamlyn Foundation and the BFI. A film version can be found on the Spoken Word Lammas YouTube Channel.

'Games' by Rahmoan Williams of Lammas School & Sixth Form won the National Poetry Society Short Poem competition in March 2017. It is published on their website: poetrysociety.org. uk/poems/games

The front cover was designed by Ben Fagan. As it is a sister book, it references the background from the *Still Falling* cover which was designed by Sonia Mijatov.

Thanks to Ben Fagan for the front cover, the support and the constant encouragement.

Thanks to all the students and teachers at the Orion and Goldbeaters primary schools, in particular Stephanie Moritz and Chris Flathers. Never have I met a head teacher with such an amazing reputation. I put it down to his sense of fun, his passion and his complete and utter respect for every student, teacher and visiting poet.

Thanks to the students and teachers at Lammas School & Sixth Form, especially Ronald Pillay and Shona Ramsey. These teachers work against all odds, often under unbelievable pressure, to support the students that need it most. This school has heart and has taught me so much about what it is to be human.

Thanks to the students, tutors and admin team at the National Youth Drama School of New Zealand, in particular Claire Keys and Michael Howard. NYDS is everyone's creative place. Thank you for providing a stray British poet with a soft landing. This kind of community is the reason I keep doing what I do.

Thank you to Clive Birnie at Burning Eye Books for handing back some of my poems for republication and to Jenn Hart, Harriet Evans and Bx3 for making this happen. Also thank you to the Roald Dahl Museum and Story Centre and to the Museum of London, to Cat Brogan, Jacob Sam-La Rose, Vicky

Macleroy and Goldsmiths University for giving me the tools to work with these young people, and to every student in every workshop for giving me inspiration, energy and purpose.

Last but by no means least, thank you to the students who gave me their permission to use their work in this collection. You are all at varying stages of life and career but every single one of you is a poet in my eyes. I have loved working with you all and do not consider this my book. I consider it ours. Thank you for your words. They are loud and will travel further than you can imagine.

Lightning Source UK Ltd.
Milton Keynes UK
UKOW05f1604120717
305175UK00002B/533/P